Voices Of Our Own

Mothers, Daughters, and Elders of the Tenderloin Tell Their Stories

Nancy Deutsch

San Francisco, California

Special thanks
This book is made possible through the generous contributions of Stone Yamashita; Mercy Housing, Inc; The Madison 4-the-Arts Fund; and Barbara and William Deutsch.

Note to readers
It has been our intent to retain the original syntax and vernacular of those whose oral histories and writings appear in this book. In this way we can truly "hear" their voices.

© 2001 by Nancy Deutsch. Printed in the United States of America. All rights reserved, including the right to reproduce this book or portions thereof in any form. Contributors maintain individual copyright for their own material. For information, contact Nancy Deutsch, 267 Fair Oaks Street, San Francisco, California 94110; email nancydeutsch@earthlink.net.

First Edition
ISBN: 0-9715320-0-1

Design by Michael Braley
Cover Photograph by Kathrin Miller
Production by Kelly St. John
Copy editing by Priscilla Jane Frank

FROM MY WINDOW

Ellen Gallagher
Elder

From my window
What a world I see. . . .

The people are the same as everywhere.
Each telling a different story—their own.
Listening to the noises—

What's going on out there? Is it a drug deal?
Is it friendly fire?
Could it be a quiet footstep for love?

ACKNOWLEDGMENTS

To the women and girls of the Tenderloin who trusted me on that frightening journey of putting their words, their lives on paper—I thank you for your courage and your friendship.

My deep gratitude goes out to the book angels who appeared at exactly the right moment and who generously gave of their time and talents: Marta Drury, Janie Frank, Russell Gardner, Dick Goldberg, Linda Joy Kattwinkel, Sandra Martz, Kathrin Miller, Jerry Sontag, and Deanne Stone.

Thanks to the California Arts Council/National Endowment for the Arts for supporting the Voices of Our Own writing program and to Winona Addison, John Chan, Sister Patsy Harney, and Gwen Yaeger, who each contributed to the richness of that program. Thanks also to the staff of 201 Turk Street Apartments.

The extraordinary circle of women who surrounded me with the endless encouragement, hope, and humor necessary to complete this book include my friends Sheila Balter, Kathy Barrows, Karen Brown, Julie Deutsch, Janie Frank, Susie Gardner, Gail Jacob, and Lisa Munro.

I wish to thank my mother, a social worker and my father, a farmer—both activists for social justice—for raising me to believe that all women should have voices of their own. At times they probably wished I hadn't taken them so seriously.

This book would never have come to fruition without the endless support of my life partner Rich Gross, whose mantra, "piece by piece," kept moving me forward against all odds. I must also thank our 10-year-old son Zack, a sensitive soul, who brought me many an early morning latte, especially that one in the redwoods.

And finally I bow to my grandmother, Evelyn Pearson, who wrote poetry, taught in Africa, and is probably the reason why I've always loved to listen to my elders.

Artists make our world colorful, provocative and noisy. They give us ideas to contemplate, capture moments in time and enrich our lives. From the work of the great masters such as Mozart and O'Keefe to the simple finger painting drawings of a child, artists touch our hearts.

Mercy Housing provides people with a safe place to discover the talents that make them unique and special. We build an attractive and affordable place where they can live and find economic stability. Then, together with the residents, we create a supportive and nurturing environment where residents can work toward building a better life for themselves and their families.

One way we help people prepare for the future is through arts programs. We were pleased to host the Voices of Our Own writing program designed specifically for the generations of women living at Mercy Housing's 111 Jones Street in San Francisco, CA. Here the culturally diverse neighborhood includes immigrants from Russia, Southeast Asia, Vietnam, China, the Philippines and Central America.

The artists in this book range in age from 7 to 77 and their stories express struggle, joy and wisdom rooted in the experience of civil war, famine and immigrant dislocation. *Voices of Our Own* has empowered these women to navigate these challenging issues and has helped them realize self-worth, overcome cultural differences, bridge generations and build a community.

Mercy Housing is committed to creating and strengthening healthy communities, and this book provides these voices a permanent home. We are honored to be a part of this book and invite you to enjoy the eloquent, moving work of the women and girls of 111 Jones Street.

FROM MERCY HOUSING

Sister Lillian Murphy, RSM
President and
Chief Executive Officer
Mercy Housing, Inc.

**MERCY HOUSING'S
111 JONES STREET
APARTMENTS**

Photograph by Kathrin Miller

Photograph by Kathrin Miller

INTRODUCTION

Nancy Deutsch

"I believe in a voice for those who have no voice." I'm driving to work in the Tenderloin after dropping off my son at school, when I hear poet Adrienne Rich on the radio. She's talking about women as witnesses and the need for poets to speak out against these dark times. I reach across the seat and grab my journal, trying not to hit the man crossing in the middle of Golden Gate and Jones. I need her words today.

I've been keeping this journal ever since I started teaching writing to women and girls in the Tenderloin. The Tenderloin, or the "TL" as the kids call it, is a community with the highest concentration of poverty in San Francisco. A neighborhood blighted by pimps, peep shows, and needles. A neighborhood that feeds on the exploitation of women. It's also a neighborhood rich in stories of struggle, survival, hope, and humor.

This isn't my first experience in the Tenderloin. Almost ten years ago I drove down this exact street. I had just moved to San Francisco from Wisconsin in my own quest to transform from social worker to writer. But first I needed a job. The newspaper ad had called for a social worker at St. Anthony's soup kitchen. The address led me to the corner of Golden Gate and Jones. Hundreds of men and a few women lined the street waiting for a free meal. There were porno shops on every corner, men lying under ragged blankets or no blankets, old women wandering the street screaming like they were possessed by demons. I leaned over to check the address; then I rolled up the windows, locked the doors, and drove on by.

Today, my class begins at 11:00 and people are just starting to line up for meals at St. Anthony's. At the front of the line, a man sits reading a dog-eared novel that I've seen him also use as a pillow. No longer afraid of making eye contact, I smile at him as I park my car in front of 111 Jones, an attractive red-brick building with a shiny new copper roof. Most of the families that live in this model of affordable housing are recent immigrants or struggling African American households. Over 11 different languages are spoken in the building, and families from Managua to Manila call this home.

My job here now, as an Artist in Residence, is to teach writing and oral history to women and girls who live in the building or the neighborhood. My students are mothers and grandmothers, for whom English is a second language, and their daughters who view writing as a subtle form of torture.

Before going to my class, I turn up the radio for the last few morsels of Adrienne Rich's inspiration. "You cannot separate poetry from the social context of human dignity and hope." OK, Adrienne, OK. But I'm only halfway through my residency and I could use a bit of hope myself these days. My students have survived war, famine, homelessness, even the death of family members, yet the war at home continues. Last week, bullets sprayed the streets and the girls told me they saw it all from their windows. "One hit our building," 12-year-old Flor tells me.

It was one of those days when I needed someone to remind me of the value of poetry in the middle of such chaos. Virginia Woolf insisted that a woman needs a room of one's own to write. My students barely have a room, much less a voice of their own, to help them survive the madness outside their windows. Between pushing the girls to write when they'd rather be listening to rap, and the daily undertow of life in the Tenderloin, I was wondering if I should get a job as a bank teller.

Over the next five years, their voices, their words, their writing would save me, inspire me, and—just when I'd be walking the plank of despair—make me smile.

Take the spunky voice of 12-year-old Anh, an honor roll student born in Vietnam whose parents spoke almost no English, who would write:

People say
Every girl should
Act like a lady
Be polite
Never be active in sports
Look skinny . . .
It does not matter what girls look like, but what's inside that counts . . .
Girls need to
speak out
so their
voices
are heard.

Or Emma, a 70-year-old Russian immigrant who'd huff and puff through class—cursing the difficulty of learning English as a grandmother—only to write in her "Dreams for My Neighborhood" poem:

In my dreams I see mothers
who never bury their sons.
I see an earth
with no borders.
In my dreams I see all races
and colors together.

I'd be delighted by "creative mistakes" made by students writing in English as a second language—cracking language open to reveal fresh images and meaning. Take for example Jean Hui Shih's letter to the governor: "I don't know anything about political . . . but please don't break our American Dream."

HOME

Painting by Anita Jones
Age 8

I'd be buoyed by the righteous indignation of Violeta and Aireen, teenagers who came to class one day with their own rap poem. The opening lines became the anthem of both the boys and the girls:

> Don't judge me by my skin
> Don't judge me by my race
> Judge me by who I am
> A person without hate . . .
> I see people staring at me
> As if I were just another piece
> Of garbage laying in the street.
> But what they don't know
> Is the real me
> A girl with a future ahead
> A girl that's sweet.

And then there was Arwa,* my most reluctant student, who crossed barriers and borders most of us cannot imagine. When we first met I thought she was much older than me, only to find out we were exactly the same age. But, Arwa had the first of three children from an arranged marriage at 15; I had my one son at 37.

For most of Arwa's life, she had lived under the veil in her native Yemen. Unlike her brothers, she was not allowed to go to school or leave the house without the escort of her father. Now in her forties, she stopped wearing the mandatory black veil of her country and started her life over in the Tenderloin.

Even with my pleading, Arwa had dropped out of the women's writing class, terribly unsure of her English. For weeks she'd been inviting me to come to her apartment to see her daughter's recent wedding pictures. As Arwa left her living room to get the photos, I stared out of her second-floor window overlooking the corner of Golden Gate and Jones. Outside, a woman in a black silver-studded bra and shorts roller-skated up and down the line of people waiting for food at St. Anthony's. Inside was a very different world—decoupage photos of Mecca on the walls, a mat where Arwa prayed five times a day, and her big-screen TV. Continually tuned to an Arabic station, on mute, her television was a sort of electronic umbilical cord to her homeland.

Arwa, her face framed by one of the many colorful silk scarves she never went without, opened the thick white photo album. Her daughter was dressed in a traditional green sequined gown from Yemen, a smiling Arwa at her side. "Your dress is beautiful. Is it from Yemen?" "No," she laughed, "from Macy's."

Learning from both the courage and contradictions of Arwa's life—and the lives of so many others I came to know—I kept teaching, and more importantly was tutored by the mothers, daughters, and elders of the Tenderloin.

One of the last things Arwa wrote in class, and with a great deal of pride, were these lines:

> When I was young, I had to wear
> a veil.
> Now that I'm older, I can walk
> alone in the Tenderloin.

If Arwa can find a voice of her own and the courage to recreate home in the Tenderloin, the least we must do is act as witness to that courage. By listening to the voice of the voiceless, we lift the veil and let in the light for change.

---

*Name changed by request.

The works in this chapter describe everyday life in the "TL" as the teenagers call the Tenderloin neighborhood of San Francisco. Many of the poems begin with the line "From My Window" or "Growing Up in the Tenderloin," which I suggested to start off the students' writing. It is clear from their words that living in the Tenderloin is not only what outsiders see—broken glass, homelessness, drugs, and despair. To the mothers, daughters, and elders who live here, the Tenderloin is also the community they are creating from scratch—a community evolving across cultures, age, and accent.

"From My Window"

CHAPTER ONE

HOMELESS WOMAN

Painting by Ellen Gallagher Elder

CHRISTMAS PARTY

Journal Entry
by Nancy Deutsch

Wonderfully strange smell of pine in the Tenderloin tonight. It overpowers the usual stench of urine that can still stop my breath. The eyes of two Cambodian girls, whose parents are Buddhists, light up when they see a huge Christmas tree being carried into the building. "Christmas is for everyone," the Irish building manager assures them. A local accounting firm has donated a Santa Claus. The kids huddle around this man who must look to them like Buddha in pj's. Santa can't pronounce the Vietnamese kids' names and keeps pulling up his fake beard, but the kids indulge this ritual and are thrilled with their gifts. Ruby says the leather backpack is "hellah better" than she expected and Trang knows she's gotten shoes but won't open them until Christmas. After the party it's dark, and as I leave the building the cops have two men and a woman up against the wall—arms and legs stretched out like snow angels. Only, angels seem out of place on the streets tonight, this night of Christmas in the Tenderloin.

CHRISTMAS IN THE TENDERLOIN

Jean Hui Shih
Elder

Christmas in the Tenderloin. Year in and year out.
A huge Christmas tree is starting to get decorated in
the center of Union Square. Its bright beauty is outstanding.
All the luxury, charm, and joy fill the area.

On the other hand, only a few blocks away is the
Tenderloin. Dirty, nasty, poor, ugly, dark shadow
throughout the Tenderloin area.

Somewhere you can see the Christmas decorations,
but it doesn't make the area look any more beautiful
or better. Like people staying in the desert, drying up,
it just looks funny. It's a shame.

I don't make fun of the Tenderloin in the season of
Christmas and New Year. I have new wishes and hope
that people don't forget the Tenderloin.
Put more concern in the Tenderloin.
Save the Tenderloin.

WISH LIST

Jasmine
Age 9

> I wish for my neighborhood to be cleaner. I wish for my mom and dad to get back together. I wish for my country to be better. My families from Yemen.
>
> Jasmine

Photograph by Kathrin Miller

"I'm a hard-struggling, positive-thinking black woman who's just tryin' to make it, tryin' to take care of my kids." VENITTA LEWIS

Venitta is the kind of woman who makes you swear you'll never complain about your own problems again. She's overcome so many obstacles, climbed out of so many crises, and still she keeps going with the determination of a locomotive. Having recovered from her own addiction, she now helps other women put their lives back together through her work at a drug treatment center. Living in the Tenderloin poses particular problems for Venitta, as some of the same women she left behind are still shooting up on the street outside her window.

VENITTA LEWIS

Oral History
by Nancy Deutsch

I was pregnant with Donisha, my third child. At that particular time I was using drugs, crack, very, very bad. Why I was using, I don't know. I just got caught up in that cycle of tryin' to fit in with the crowd, tryin' to follow my kid's father.

When I found out I was pregnant, it still didn't stop. I kept on doin' it, doin' it, doin' it. And one day I did it, and I did it so much that I took a hit and my back busted out. Just like that. I got in the hospital, like maybe 20 minutes later, and by the time the doctor came in, Donisha was here. That's how quick. I was about 25.

Durin' this time, I already had reports on me, 'cause my family was tired of it. They was really concerned about the kids. At the time, Felicia was maybe four, if that. And Freddie was two. It was very hard; I had my hands full. It was a tragedy. So, as soon as she was born, the kids was taken. They was taken from me. First they went to my mother, but she couldn't handle it, 'cause it was too many kids. Plus she had Donisha and Donisha was born positive [for drugs]. So they went into foster homes. I had to get myself into recovery, get myself together.

Donisha went through some seizures, she went through a lot of withdrawals, a lot of shakes. And I wasn't there most of this time, it was too hard for me. I mean, you talk about a good excuse to run and get high, it was one of the best ones. I tried that, but it was still killin' me up inside. I knew I loved my children no matter what, so I had to get myself together. By then they said Donisha was gonna be retarded.

She was in therapy for years, she couldn't get potty-trained, I mean she finally started getting better when she was four. Little by little, you know, she started growin' up. She's really turned out to be a winner. She blossomed. She's not in handicapped class or anything like that. She's an honor roll student. She loves me a lot. She's like a blessing. She's like a blessing from God.

I moved [to 111 Jones] in June of '93, right when it opened. I was so happy because I was livin' in a transitional house for mothers and kids. At the time I could only have Donald with me, my youngest son. I was workin' down here [in the Tenderloin] as a home care aide and I just put in an application one day. I was tryin' anything 'cause I knew I needed a place.

When I finally walked in the door, I was just crying away. I was all by myself. I was like, "Thank you, God," because I had finally got me an apartment. I only had Donald and as soon as I got in I called Child Protective Services. The worker came out here and boom—Felicia and Fred was home, maybe three weeks later.

Donisha was a little bit harder because they had to decide, can I do it all—can I really raise these kids, go to work, do what I'm supposed to do, take the kids to school, can I really do it? The lady wanted to make sure I could really take care of them, 'cause this would be the first time I'd ever really taken care of four kids by myself, and doin' it right without makin' all kinds of terrible mistakes. But, I did it. I got 'em all in school, too.

VENITTA LEWIS AND DAUGHTER FELICIA

Photograph by Kathrin Miller

I'm a resident manager at a residential treatment center now, full-time. I take care of women who are tryin' to keep themselves clean and sober. I watch over them, make sure they're doing the right things. Guide them, talk to them about drugs. A lot of them are mothers in recovery and have had their kids taken away from them. I have been there and I know all about it.

The hardest thing in raising my daughters here is the drugs. You can't even walk down the street without seein' somebody takin' a hit off a crack pipe! There's girls, like my daughter's age and they sellin' out there. No older than my daughter! Their parents are probably on drugs. The cycle goes round and round. I don't want my daughters to get into that. I'm tryin' to protect my kids. I don't want them to be caught up in the cycle that I was into. Hopefully, they just all grow up, be OK, go to college. Felicia's the oldest in the house. She wants to be a lawyer, 'cause she likes to argue. Hopefully, she'll be that.

I'd like to go back to school, maybe study computers. My mother just did. If she can do it, I know I can do it. I'm a hard-struggling, positive-thinking black woman who's just tryin' to make it, tryin' to take care of my kids.

Photograph by Kathrin Miller

FROM MY WINDOW

Myrna McDonald
Age 17

From my window I hear
voices that need help
a child that's helpless and abandoned
by the person they love.

From my window I see blood
an innocent person at the wrong
place at the wrong time.

From my window I hear
a cry, a newborn coming into
this world.

From my window I feel lost
it's hard to find somebody to
love when you need it.

From my window I wonder
what's gonna happen in the
next few minutes in the next
few minutes, oh I wonder
what's gonna happen in the
next few minutes.

GROWING UP IN THE TENDERLOIN

Ana Perez
Age 14

Growing up in the Tenderloin is fun because I met lots of friends from different races—Russians, African-Americans, Chinese, Japanese, Vietnamese, Filipinos, Cambodians, and more Latinos. I am glad that I moved here because I feel that I am more into the community and that I got a chance to know other cultures, especially when we have our potlucks. I try different foods and I enjoy them and I take some of our Latino foods so that others can enjoy them. That's why I like living in the Tenderloin. Of course, being in this poetry class is the funnest because in writing journals and writing poetry I can express my feelings in many ways.

LIVING IN THE TENDERLOIN

Ruby Marucut
Age 10

Living in the Tenderloin is fun because there's classes and you could meet a lot of friends and you could go to some of the activities like the art class and more. There's a playground and a lot of kids play there. But, mostly the girls' writing is more fun for me.

LIVING IN THE TENDERLOIN

Sita Meas
Age 9

Living in the Tenderloin is fun because we have classes and food and also we have friends to play with and that's why living in the Tenderloin is fun.

UNTITLED

Painting by Ciceila Khorn
Age 9

UNTITLED

Anonymous

I WISH

Tina Eat
Age 10

I wish for my neighborhood to be good.
I wish all children had a safe neighborhood
where they could walk with their heads up and could feel safe.
I wish there were no homeless in the Tenderloin.
I wish that my native country, Cambodia, won't be poor!
I wish for a Walkman.

I don't feel safe in this neighborhood because of all the alcoholics and drug users. That's not good. If I had a wish it would be to have cleaner streets and less homeless, drug users and alcoholics. I don't feel safe out there, but I feel safe in here in my building with people I trust and care about and I know they care about me too, like my mother does. If I had a million dollars I would separate it in half. Half for my university account and half to build homeless shelters for homeless people and so the streets would be cleaner.

What would you use it for?

Think about it.

GROWING UP IN THE TENDERLOIN

Flor Beltran
Age 12

STREET

Photograph by Flor Beltran
Age 12

Raindrops fall, millions Dashing on the windowpane Each one an image.

HAIKU

Adelle Pierce
Elder

FROM MY WINDOW

Ellen Gallagher
Elder

Looking out my window what a world I see!
Down below all the carts and more carts pushed by tired people.

Up above the sun and the sky and a little bit of hope.
Always hope.
The smells—musty pollution.
Buildings faded with years.

The people are the same as everywhere.
Each telling a different story—their own.
Listening to the noises—

What's going on out there? Is it a drug deal?
Is it friendly fire?
Could it be a quiet footstep for love?

Photograph by Kathrin Miller

UNTITLED

Photograph by Flor Beltran
Age 12

LIFE AND DEATH

Ana Perez
Age 14

Life is a thermometer
filled with ups and downs
what will happen tomorrow
you never know what will happen
when you are walking around the
town.

Death is pain
it comes when you least expect it
falling from the sky is rain
taking your hopes and dreams in
one chain
there is nothing we can do to stop it.

Love is a rainbow of four colors
black is bringing the pain
white is bringing the happiness
red is bringing the love
and purple is bringing the madness.

Death is sadness
sadness like a gun
when I look at it, it makes me cry
knowing that weapon takes away
people's lives,
but one day this world will end so
don't just
wait there for it to end because
there is more
in between what we call life and
death.

**THE TENDERLOIN IS
A STALKING CHEETAH**

Group poem by
Women's Writing Class
Betti, Ellen, Emma, Jean,
Marilia and Yolanda
Ages 53–74

The Tenderloin is a stalking cheetah,
bad mouths and bad streets that never sleep.
The Tenderloin is forgotten cats and dogs
dead flowers, empty Coke bottles
tired feet and trash in the street.

The Tenderloin is murky brown
dark misty, streaks of red blood
reeks of urine and too many wasted lives.

The Tenderloin is rap, rock, pop
a desperate wail, a constant breathing
to get one pure breath.

The Tenderloin is blue skies, fluffy clouds,
golden sunshine, beautiful music
street art, action, truth, life!

The Tenderloin is cheap rent,
where my family lives,
the best place for me,
the Tenderloin is home.

The Tenderloin is a stalking cheetah,
bad mouths and bad streets, that never sleep.
The Tenderloin is where every day
I can see a movie without a ticket.

FROM MY WINDOW

Betty Miner
Mother

From my window I see gulls
lined up and sitting on street lamps
like many sentinels. Their mew-mew
cries to one another as they dive
for bread thrown from passersby.

From my window I see the line
at St. Anthony's Dining Room
getting longer and longer each day.
I hear the various conversations of
those in line, the mixture makes a
sound as of a beehive of activity.
Some voices are loud, some softer.

The smells of the homeless reek
on our streets, they huddle in
doorways and alleys with their
shopping carts full of meager
belongings.

I hear the screaming of sirens as
they drive by our building, police,
fire engines, and ambulances. This
neighborhood throbs of activity
and never sleeps.

Sometimes in the evenings, the
night is split with multivoiced
car alarms the #5 Fulton sets off.
People call out to one
another
in the night,
they scream and curse.

Photograph by Bill McLeod

"OH, WOW, YOU LIVE IN THE TENDERLOIN?"

Group poem by Girls' Writing Class
Amy, Angela, Romany and Sita
Ages 9–12

The Tenderloin is a good place and bad place
a festival, a playground,
a place you can get
pregnant.

The Tenderloin is cool, broken,
happy, sad, sometimes bad,
sometimes shootings
and other things that hurt.

The Tenderloin is black, yellow,
green, so many different people around.
The Tenderloin is blue,
blue, the color of the sky.

The Tenderloin is garbage cans and weed,
rap and sounds of nature
hot, cool, wonderful
when the sun rises.

The Tenderloin is always a part of us
never apart from people,
it's where I have what I need
—my family, my friends,
it's NEVER boring.

The Tenderloin is a good place and bad place
a festival, a playground
it's when you live in the "TL" people say,
"Oh, Wow! You live in the Tenderloin!"
"Oh, Wow! You LIVE in the Tenderloin?"

Photograph by Kathrin Miller

"Home Is Like A Ball That Rolls Everywhere"

CHAPTER TWO

In the five years I worked in the Tenderloin, I tried to get everyone I met to write a "Home" poem. With eleven languages spoken in the buildings and trajectories that spanned the globe, this seemed to be one way to bridge cultural barriers and learn about each other's homelands. Some of the "Home" poems were written in class, some were written on napkins at holiday parties or spoken perhaps in Arabic, Spanish, Russian, or Chinese and then later translated. We even strung them on a clothesline for the building's fourth-year anniversary party. With all the contradictions these residents navigate, it is clear that wherever home used to be—home is now the Tenderloin.

Some kids don't have homes
Some kids live in shelters
Some kids even live in the streets.
Some kids get hurt
Some kids cry
Some go home
Some kids live with their parents
Some kids live near
Some kids leave here
Others kids have homes
But, I live in the perfect one.

HOME

Mia Berry
Age 7

HOME

Painting by Janelle Panaligan
Age 9

WOMEN'S WRITING CLASS

Journal Entry
by Nancy Deutsch

Today in class, I asked Betti if she was OK, and she answered with a blunt "No." She was worried about possible SSI cuts, which would mean she and her husband would have to move out of the building. She passed out "mug rugs," to put under our coffee cups, which she had crocheted out of string collected from the street and garbage cans. We worked on our "Home" poems. Ellen wrote, "Home is like fried chicken—outer crunchy, inner guessing." Marilia, who's originally from Brazil, asked her what that meant. Ellen said, "It's like Kentucky Fried Chicken. It looks good on the outside, you have to guess what's inside. Sometimes it's good, sometimes it isn't." She tells us she never had chicken growing up. She was raised in an orphanage in Umatilla, Oregon. "I would have loved a family sitting around the Sunday table eating fried chicken."

HOME

Ellen Gallagher
Elder

Home is Umatilla, Oregon.
Home is San Francisco.
Home is like fried chicken—outer crunchy, inner guessing.
Home is like a river, forever running.
Home is warm, cozy, full of music and color.
Home is always happy as long as my cat Marmi is there to greet me.
Home is fearless and not listening to others' troubles.
Home is never having the door locked.

HOME

Ashley Adams
Age 9

Home is like candy and ice cream land.
Home is like a cold Icee.
Home is the building where I live.
Home is like banana pudding.
Home is always active.
Home is never ugly.
Home is the House of Pancakes.

Photograph by Kathrin Miller

"We had eight in our family. My sister, Alejandrina, started helping my parents when she was eight. Picking cotton. We would start working from six in the morning till five in the afternoon." VICTORIA AMADO

Photograph by Kathrin Miller

Victoria and her sister Alejandrina are a testament to the power of sisterhood. Raising Victoria's now 14-year-old son together, they are a seamless team, supporting each other through a lifetime of economic hardship. Victoria was also extremely generous in the girls' writing class. She would patiently spell out "P-E-R-U," which sounded to the teens like another planet; let the girls touch the soft llama wool she'd brought; and with characteristic humor, exhort them to stay in school. Even after 20 years in the U.S., she still carries a dream of going back to the rural countryside of her beloved Peru, "when I'm old."

VICTORIA AMADO

Oral History
by Nancy Deutsch

My parents worked on the farm, the hacienda, in Cañete. It's a village to the south of Lima, the capital of Peru. Green everyplace. We worked in the fields for a *patrón*. I remember when we were little, on Christmas, his wife used to give to all the people who worked for him a doll, and groceries, food. We had a kind of life in that village, poor, you know. But we keep good memories of those people.

We had eight in our family. My sister, Alejandrina, started helping my parents when she was eight. Picking cotton. We would start working from six in the morning till five in the afternoon.

The school was first through the fifth grade. When we had to help on the farm, we had to leave school. I was 11 when I left school, fifth grade. I wanted to go from fifth to high school. We could not afford to go more. At that age, you don't think that later you're gonna be so sorry that you didn't go to high school. But, later, you sorry.

We were poor, poor, poor, poor! Even sometimes we didn't have food to eat. Sometimes, just boiled sweet potatoes. And when we moved from the hacienda to the city it was worse! On the hacienda, there were a lot of vegetables and potatoes.

When we moved to the city, it was really bad. That's why my sister had to go to work for money at 12 years old. My parents know only farm work. My father would carry the water, cement, bricks for the construction. In our country, they don't pay good—even if you work so hard. My mother started to do the laundry for other people, by hand! I remember my mother sometimes, the middle of the night, she had pain and I would get medicine and start rubbing her hands. Then, when I was 16, my father died. And after me were four or five more children.

I came to this country for work, looking for a better opportunity. I was happy that I had an opportunity to come here, but I was sad to leave my mother, my family, my country. It wasn't easy. I don't have a high education, so I worked as a housekeeper. I wanted to finish school. But I had to start working, any kind of work, so I could start sending money to my mother.

I don't like to say this, but I felt so sad. The truth is, I felt awful. I could see everything was different from my country. There's a different culture. I was here just myself. And I missed my mother and I cry a lot. For about two years.

What did I miss about Peru? Everything. [laughs] The food! My favorite is the kind of food we make, *anticucho*—we make it by the heart of the cow. And *picarones*, very sweet. We make with sweet potatoes, squash, a little flour, a little salt. They boil it in a big pan of oil. It's a lot of work. When

Photograph by Kathrin Miller

it is ready to eat, we put syrup with some fig leaves.

I had my son, Juan Carlos, when I was 40. I never married. I was just myself. My sister Alejandrina came when he was three months old. It was really a nice experience having a child, and I have a nice son. I love him very much. Oh! He's my life. When he was one year old, Alejandrina had to go back to Peru, because my mother had cancer. She was going to die. My younger sister convinced me to stay here with my child. Alejandrina came back when Juan Carlos was ready for kindergarten. So, all those years it was really hard for me. I had to work and leave my child with somebody else.

My sister never had children, always busy helping raise other children. It's fun to be single, because nobody bosses her around. I think 25 is the best age to have children. And not 18 or 19. No, no, no! If I could have a chance to marry at 24 or 25, that's better.

My sister's thinking of going back to my country when Juan Carlos turns 20 years old. He's 14 now. I can't say the same thing, because I have my son here. If it was just myself, I would say the same thing. I wish I could go back when I'm old. I'm 54 years old now.

My sister and I have a lot of things in common. A lot. But, we are opposite in character. Growing up, I hated cooking. She hated washing dishes. We are still the same. She's so easy and I like everything perfect. That's the only thing that we always have problems with. When she see me upset and I start talking, she just turns and walks away. When she come back—I'm OK. We help each other. She helps me a lot, and I help her, too.

I've lived in the Tenderloin for 20 years. When I first moved here, the area wasn't bad, like now. When we lived on O'Farrell Street, there were a lot of those ladies, how do I say, prostitutes. A lot. And I could see that there were young people selling drugs. My apartment was very bad. Rats, cockroaches. I heard about another apartment in this building for a little bit more. The area was still bad, but the building was clean, bigger.

At the beginning, I didn't feel like I was a part of this country; then later on, I started to feel confident. Ever since I could remember, I used to see my mother and father work so hard on the farm and always it would be the same. No improvement. Here, I work hard, but I can afford to pay my rent. I can afford to have food for my family. And, you know, I have my child. I support him myself. Besides that, I could still send money to my mother. So, that's what was different. They work so hard, but always the same. I work so hard, but I can see it's different.

HOME

Flor Beltran
Age 12

Home is Diriamba, Nicaragua.
Home is 201 Turk Street, San Francisco.
Home is *gallopinto* mixed with
nicaragüense y americano.
Home is *buñuelos*, sweet with honey and good.
Home is mango trees, sunny and bright.
Home is sunflowers always looking up
to examples like parents.
Home is cool and clean rivers.
Home is a place where everyone loves
each other and shares and helps.
Home is a magic place with wonders and happiness.
Home is never a dark, black sky or clouds.
It's always a bright sunny day.

HOME

Benita Arguero
Elder

Home is San Jose City, Philippines.
Home is San Francisco.
Home is like light that gets bright and then dark.
Home is paradise.
Home is unity.
Home is always happy and busy.
Home is all members of the family living peacefully.
Home is never closed to good friends coming in.
Home is my lovely home with my family.
Home is like a ball that rolls everywhere.

MASSIEL'S HAND

Photograph by Flor Beltran
Age 12

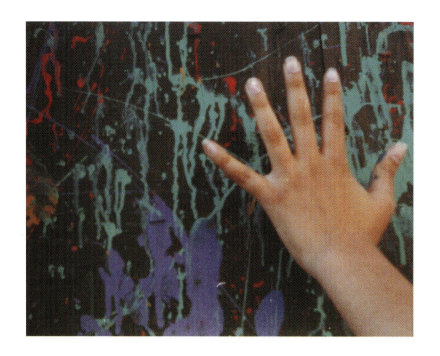

HOME

Anh Nguyen
Age 13

Home is where people of all different colors, shapes, and sizes are sewn together by a thread.

My home country is Thailand.
I left my country in 1984.
Now home is Frisco, California.
Home is a fruit that tastes so sweet.
Home is an open cloud that lets the sun come out and shine.
Home is a place where everyone shares something special together.
Home should be dignity and pride.
Home should be sweet and caring.
Home is one thing in life that will be a part of you forever.
Home is never forgotten in life.

HOME

Sophia Tana
Age 13

Home is a village in the Ukraine.
I left my home when I was one month old.
Now home is here.
Home is the place where my family is together.
Home is love and happiness.
Home should be safe and healthy.
Home is never cold and empty.
Home is always a fortress in my life.

HOME

Emma Khatsernova
Elder

Home is Granada La Gran Sultana.
Home is *aguardiente* and happiness.
Home is Lake Cocibolca, big and beautiful.
Home is sharing and the most important—love.
Home is now so empty because
my mother, my brothers and sisters are not here.
Home is always love, devotion, emotion.
Home is never bad memories.
Home is the best memories blessed.

HOME

Nidia Urbina
Mother

HOME

Painting by Linda Nguyen
Age 7

HOME

Loura Soun
Age 11

Home is a royal kingdom
that strange people don't really know.
Home is a big, whole chicken that cannot fall apart.
Home is a California poppy
that always will be open and loves each other heart to heart.
Home is a metal that can lock or unlock,
that can't break or bend.
Home is the shelter for us and you.
Home should be your admirer and don't let go
whatever you can do.
Home is always the thing you need forever.
Home is never a wrong place, but can make you
feel better.
Home is anything, everywhere, any place
you see the smiling faces.

MY SPECIAL PLACE

Violeta Perez
Age 17

My special place is my room.
My room is my special place because
there is peace, quiet, and it is calm
when I am in it.

I like to do my homework in my
special place because when I am there
I can concentrate.
My mind forgets about the things
that are around me and I just think
about what I'm doing.

When I am mad I go to my special place.
I think that if I go there I can forget
about my madness and just turn the
madness into a quiet happiness.

I hope that I could show someone
my special place so that they know
how it feels to have a special place like mine.
Maybe if I tell other people about my
special place they can make their own
But I think that I will keep the secret a little longer.

HOME

Yolanda Bove
Elder

It is very sad to leave
your native country and go to the other country
where we meet many bad
surprises and a future unknown.
Tears and sorrow flow from my
heart when I remember the past
and all the castles I built falling down.
Now there is only dust.

MY HOMETOWN

Group poem by Women's Writing Class
Adelle, Benita, Betti and Felisa
Ages 53–74

My hometown is Jaen Neva Ecija
Dink Town, Texas
Cardston, Canada
San Jose City, Philippines.

In my hometown I see mango trees,
a big cloud of peat dirt,
a white marble temple,
sweet, brown *chico*.

In my hometown I smell the bad odor of the neighbor's pigs,
manure from 300 chickens,
oil roads on gravel,
pine trees in the wind.

In my hometown I hear crickets in the night,
crickets in the night,
crickets in the night,
crickets and frogs in the night.

Home is Winiya, Ukraine.
I left my home in 1992.
Home is always Alexandra and Ellen.
Home is like chicken.
Home is like a rose.
Home should be good.
Home is never war.

HOME

Sura Maptynov
Elder

**WOMEN FROM YEMEN
IN COURTYARD**

Photograph by Gwen Yaeger

Home is Ibb, Yemen.
Home is like baklava.
Home is like a peach tree.
Home is green.
Home is like the mountains of my country.
Home is happy.
Home should be like nice weather.
Home is my family.

HOME

Arwa Farhan
Mother

HOME

Esperanza Castañeda
Mother

Home is Guadalajara, Mexico.
Home is *pozole, tamales, enchiladas*.
Home is Lake Chapala, when the
sun is shining.
Home is blue, like Lake Chapala.
Home is all my family together.

HOME

Siomara Castañeda
Age 8

Home is Guadalajara, Mexico.
Home is like chow mein.
Home is like a yellow rose,
my favorite color.
Home is sometimes a river
eating a plant.
Home is a sunflower smiling.

HOME

Rossana Alonzo
Mother

Home is Granada, Nicaragua, where I was raised.
My home is where I come from and find love
every day after work.
My home is where my daughter and sister
are sleeping every night.
Home is like rice and beans to me.
Home is like a beautiful afternoon,
when it's neither hot nor cold.
Home is my little place where I can be me,
no dressing up, no pretending.
Home is always where you can really be you.
Home is never where you feel uncomfortable.
Home is where my mom is.
Home is where I live.

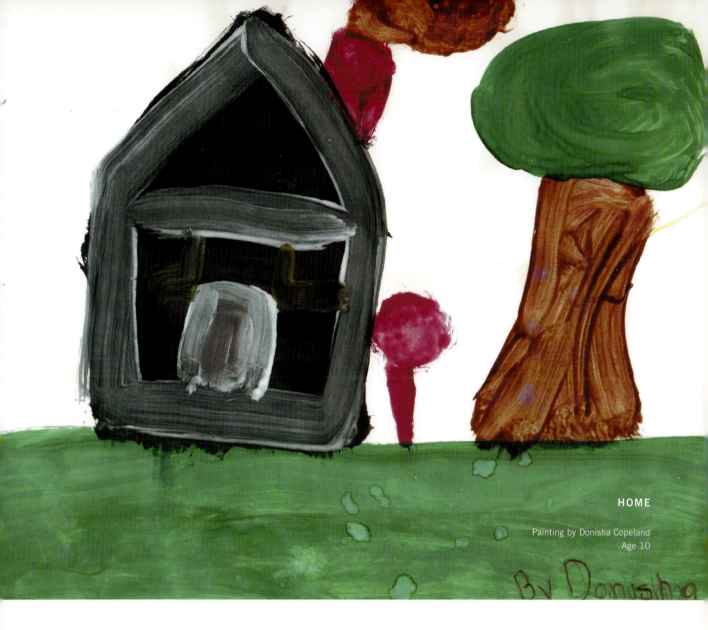

HOME

Painting by Donisha Copeland
Age 10

HOME

Stephanie Phan
Age 12

My home was Vietnam.
I left my home in 1988.
Now home is 201 Turk Street.
Home is like lemon on a pie.
Home is a bunch of willow trees.
Home is a school of fish.
Home is always a big rain forest.
Home is purple.
Home is filled with almond cookies.
Home is never on drugs.

CHAPTER THREE

"I Seem To Be A Broken Heart, But Really I'm A Shining Emerald"

This line was written in a style I call "poetry on the run." The girls would come in after school, tired and not at all interested in anything that smacked of homework. They would balk, banter, French braid my hair—anything to keep from writing. But when they would write, it was often as compelling as this line by Aireen. The "I Seem To Be" poems stem from Kenneth Koch's work with inner-city children. The words of the Tenderloin girls vibrate with boldness and ambivalence as they tackle issues of cultural pride, gender, and the tumultuous emotions of adolescence. Of course, they also wanted to write about love, loneliness, and their singing idol Selena.

AIREEN WITH FAMILY PHOTOS

Photograph by Angela Zamora
Age 12

I seem to be a broken heart,
but really I'm a shining emerald.
I seem to be a fragile glass,
but really I'm as hard as metal.
I'm Aireen.
I am your neighbor.

I SEEM TO BE

Aireen Bulante
Age 12

GIRLS' WRITING CLASS

Journal Entry
by Nancy Deutsch

Anh, one of the Vietnamese girls, came into class after school selling Easter candy. The last time I saw her, she sold me tiny silver earrings which I've yet to find an owner for. "My school has a lot of fund-raisers," she apologized, adding that the social worker and I are her best customers. I agreed to go for the chocolate malted milk ball eggs if she would stay and write with us in class. "Every girl should . . ." was our writing topic for the night. Anh said, "You mean like girls are supposed to be sugar and spice and everything nice? I think this world's very sexist!" I admire her outrage as well as her entrepreneurial spirit. Romany, who rarely comes to class—and when she does it's for five minutes before bolting—seems to be compelled enough by the topic to try writing also. She told us her Cambodian parents still believe in arranged marriages. "They say if you're fat, they won't be able to marry you off. I don't want no damn husband anyway!" Then, as quickly as she entered, she tossed her paper my way asking when she could put her poem on the computer. I consider this a victory.

EVERY GIRL SHOULD

Anh Nguyen
Age 12

People say
Every girl should
Act like a lady
Be polite
Never be active in sports
Look skinny
Never overeat.

I think this is sexist.
It does not matter what girls look like,
but what's inside that counts.
Their personality, character, thoughts,
and feelings are what counts and
should matter!

Girls need to
speak out
so their
voices
are heard.

Photograph by Kathrin Miller

"My necklace is gold, with my initial in Cambodian. If something happens, I sell it back. Mostly, the Cambodian families try to save a lot of gold. When a war comes they sell it back to get money to escape. For freedom. That's why I want to buy gold. I don't know, maybe in the future, maybe something happen."

VEN YEM MEAS

"Just like in The Killing Fields,*" begins Ven's 28-year-old son, who acted as translator. "Did you see the movie? In real life it's worse than that." Ven Yem Meas lost almost everything when the ruthless Khmer Rouge invaded Cambodia. Now she has started her life over in the Tenderloin. Like so many immigrant mothers, Ven is caught between worlds—that of her teenage daughters, who walk daily through the war zones of the Tenderloin, and the traditions and memories of the Cambodia she fled. Despite the death and devastation Ven witnessed, she has an amazing resilience, a warm smile, and an easy laugh that was salvaged by the grace of some god. Whenever I see her, she grabs my hand and repeats over and over, "Akun, akun," thanking me for the generosity she's received in this country.*

I'm 58 years old. I was born and raised in Cambodia, in a small village called Battanbang. I raised 14 children, but only nine are left. The oldest one, my daughter Savuong, is still in Cambodia. Five of my children died from the Khmer Rouge, from being hungry. Most of them were starving and some killed by the Khmer Rouge. My mother and father died from the Khmer Rouge.

When I was young, my mother and father had a small family farm. Later, my father became an army soldier. We were poor. My mother and I still worked on the farm. We raised pigs. We grew orange, apple, mango, corn, vegetables, rice. Before the Khmer Rouge we had a garden, a whole block. It was hard work. The sun hits you hard, your back hurts. The water from the rice hits you to your knees. We smashed the rice with a wooden block. After you smash it, you throw it to the air and let the shell fly out. Only the rice is left.

I didn't have time to go to school. I never learned to read. I had to raise my sisters too. We used a lamp, no electricity. Only in the city, they had electricity. And the water, we get from the river. The closest city was Phnom Penh. I never went to the city when I was a girl. I wanted to go but I couldn't afford. I had no money.

I married at 19. In our culture, in Cambodia, we don't have boyfriend or girlfriend. When the girl is a little bit bigger than Sophonn [Ven's daughter], when she's 18, the engagement is arranged. For girl, you stay home, cook, you help your parents, don't go out. From 12 to 17 you cannot walk with a boy. If they find out you walked with a boy, they whip you with a stick. They're strict with the children. Not like here.

My husband and I never met before he came to my house. It's up to the parents, if the parents like the man. I had never seen him before that day. I was scared and nervous. I never met a boy before or held a boy's hand or anything.

We lived with my parents. The Khmer Rouge had been in the country maybe seven or eight months, then my parents were killed in 1975. My mother starved. They only feed you one scoop of rice and the rest was just water from the soup. My father was killed, smashed in the head with a stick because he was a soldier.

The Khmer Rouge would come during the day or at night while everyone was sleeping. They lined up the whole village at gunpoint and questioned everyone. Anyone who disagree with them or disobey their orders was beaten or killed. My husband was beaten several times.

VEN YEM MEAS

Oral History
by Nancy Deutsch
Translated from Cambodian
by her son Vuth Meas

Photograph by Kathrin Miller

When my daughter Vath was born, they made me go back to work in the farm, after three days, in the rain. I was bleeding; I was in water up to my knees. I worked from 5:00 in the morning to noon, then eat one scoop of rice, then work till the night.

I gave some of my food to my children. I'd rather starve myself. When I was hungry, I ask for some rice and the Khmer Rouge said no. I felt inside, "I grew it, why can't I get some?" So, I just go steal it. They came and chopped my nose with a knife. They hit me in my head.

We escaped from Cambodia in 1979 to Thailand refugee camp. The Khmer Rouge had a war with the Vietnamese, so we left. We ran at nighttime to Thailand camp. Halfway, we met the Vietnamese soldiers and they protect us, they let us come to Thailand camp. At the time it was my husband and me and five of my children. Lots of people fled. It took about four days. We walked. We slept in the jungle, then we walk again.

We were in three different refugee camps in Thailand and then one in the Philippines. My other two sons were born in refugee camps. We were admitted to the United States as refugees in 1983.

I want to thank your country, your culture, for all they do for us, for helping us. Before we lived in this apartment, we lived across the street. But, the apartment had rats, roaches. I itched all over from fleas. I like it here [111 Jones Street]. Here, it's clean. It's safe. There's a garden. I like all the flowers.

I want my children to be good, get an education, and listen to their parents—not go out. You come to the United States and your children don't listen. I don't want them to have boyfriends. In our culture, if you're a woman, you only go out with your parents. You have to stay close to your Mom and learn things about the house, how to do things for your husband. But if they're not around they can't learn.

Every time I hear about the Khmer Rouge, I feel bad. It's hard to remember. My necklace is gold, with my initial in Cambodian. If something happens, I sell it back. Mostly, the Cambodian families try to save a lot of gold. When a war comes they sell it back to get money to escape. For freedom. That's why I want to buy gold. I don't know, maybe in the future, maybe something happen.

I seem to be a mirror,
But really I'm just a reflection.

I SEEM TO BE

Felicia Copeland
Age 12

Photograph by Kathrin Miller

I seem to be the pillars
Of the strongest structure,
But really I'm the stitching
That keeps the seams together.

I SEEM TO BE

Winona Addison
Mother

SUN, MOON

Painting by Ashley Adams
Age 9

I SEEM TO BE

Ashley Adams
Age 9

I seem to be the sun, but really I'm the moon.
I seem to be a tiger, but really I'm a lion.
I seem to be a cat, but really I'm a dog.
I seem to be pretty, but really I'm beautiful.

I SEEM TO BE

Myrna McDonald
Age 14

I seem to be an innocent kitten,
But really I'm a black panther.
I am Myrna, the original female.

You think I'm a peaceful waterfall,
But I'm a lion, that has a lot of
Problems on my mind.

I SEEM TO BE

Violeta Perez
Age 17

I seem to be a helpless bunny,
But really I'm a Latina with power.

I SEEM TO BE

Flor Beltran
Age 12

I seem to be a calm wind,
But really I am a wild tornado.
I seem to be a bunny,
But really I am a lion.
I seem to be a beautiful rose
Surrounded by friends,
But really I am a lonely sunflower.
I seem to be a sunny, beautiful day,
But really I am an ugly, windy, stormy day.

Photograph by Kathrin Miller

I AM THE GIRL WITH THE BEAUTIFUL DRESS

Ruby Marucut
Age 11

I am spring
I am the butterfly
I am the sun
I am every kind of flower
I am the rabbit
I am the girl with a beautiful dress
I am the cloud
I am the ants and the bugs
I am a diamond ring
I am only spring.

LOVE IS

Diana Lee
Age 12

Love

is

a

tree

of

history.

LOVE IS

Jean Hui Shih
Elder

Love tastes
like sugarcane,
where you eat
from one end
to the other
getting better
over time.

LOVE IS

Felica Copeland
Age 11

Love tastes like sugar
smells like candy
is forever and ever.

Love is like a butterfly
that never flew away.

Love feels like glue so that
you can't fall apart.

The world needs a big fat heart.

LOVE IS

Klara Taran
Elder

Love is an orchid.
Love is good weather.

Love tastes like strawberries.
Love smells like when I make
gefilte fish.

Love feels like when we are happy.
Love is like my family, my
grandsons and granddaughters.

Love remembers my life when
I was a young girl going to college.
Love forgets the bad time when I
lived in Siberia.

Love is a memory of my mother
and father when they were with us
in the Ukraine.

**KLARA TARAN
AND FAMILY IN
THE UKRAINE**

CHALK ON SIDEWALK

Photograph by Ruby Marucut
Age 11

I SEEM TO BE

Ruby Marucut
Age 11

I seem to be a cactus
But really I'm a blooming rose.

I seem to be a butterfly
But really I'm a killer bee.

I seem to be the grass where people step on
But really I'm the hard ground where people step on
I am Ruby, I am your neighbor.

LONELINESS

Lena Medvedovskaya
Elder

When I came to the U.S., I felt very lonely because I didn't know English. I couldn't talk with people and I didn't have friends. All my friends I lost in Russia.
I cried all the time.

I didn't know this town and it was difficult to go to the doctor. The first time my daughter helped me and then she told me that "If every time I help you, you can never do anything." I decided to do all by myself.
I took myself in hand.

Now, I can talk a little, read an English book, use the transportation and have friends. Now, I don't feel lonely.

MERARI CASTAÑEDA

Age 13

Photograph by Kathrin Miller

IN MEMORY OF SELENA

Flor Beltran
Age 12

The day she died
everything went
Black.
Remember the good times she had.
Also the
pain.
Pain
That ran through all her friends
As family members wept on her
Coffin and
Grave.
So every time you hear her name
or songs
Remember the laughter
Shattered
Away.

BACKSTAGE

Winona Addison
Mother

When I was yo age
 Backstage
 of my life,

I took every drug
 until I dug
  a hole
  so deep
  for me

It took years to get out.
 Years of hurt.
 Years of doubt.

I didn't even know who I was
 and I knew everything.

Now as I reminisce
when I was yo age

 Backstage,
  of my life

It wasn't about no drug
 or human love.

It was about God
 in the heavens above
  who watched over me

when I was yo age
 Backstage . . . .

"When I Look Into My Mother's Eyes I See The World"

CHAPTER FOUR

Unlike the alienation that sometimes clouds the relationship between mothers and their adolescent daughters in this country, the daughters I met in the Tenderloin expressed an intense loyalty and admiration for their mothers. You can see this in the girls' poems, "My Mother's Eyes." Maybe because the girls witness the daily sacrifices of their mothers, or perhaps because of their strong cultural bonds, the chasm between generations seemed to be more easily bridged. In the women's class, I asked the students to bring in photographs of their mothers and themselves from the past and we literally wrote to the women in the pictures. We laughed together and sometimes cried as they shared mistakes of youth, memories of surviving World War II, or the cinnamon bark and lavender smells of childhood.

FELICIA

Photograph by Ruby Marucut
Age 12

I look in my mother's eyes and I see
a beautiful reflection of me and the answers
to all my questions.

I look in my mother's eyes and I see
a blue river with a rainbow going across.

I look in my mother's eyes and I see
a tiger that reminds me of how strong she is.

I look in my mother's eyes and I see
myself walking downtown shopping for her.

I look in my mother's eyes and I see a
woman who is willing to take care of her four kids
using every bit of power she has.

I look in my mother's eyes and I see
a strong, black woman
her heart covering mine with warmth
the goodness of love and the tenderness,
everything a woman could possibly want.

**MY MOTHER'S EYES,
FOR MY MOTHER
VENITTA LEWIS**

Felicia Copeland
Age 12

WOMEN'S WRITING CLASS

Journal Entry
by Nancy Deutsch

These women are definitely bonding—today in class they discussed brands of hair color in six different accents. It seems like they actually reach across the table, across cultures and language barriers to help each other tell their stories. While I tried to untangle Raya's English mixed with Russian, Yolanda, a Spanish speaker, jumped in and helped Raya find the words she needed. Haltingly, Raya told us that her father had been unfaithful. She said her mother eventually took her father back for their daughter's sake—so she would have enough money to send Raya to college. "She loved me that much," Raya said. "She taught me that your mother should be your best friend." Raya, who's now in her seventies, did eventually go to college and still considers her mother her best friend.

MY MOTHER'S EYES

Betti Miner
Mother

I look in my mother's eyes
and see her tired after work—
the smell of peaches
tanned, weathered skin
faded dress
my Sioux and Cherokee
heritage.

MY DAUGHTERS' EYES

Marilia Brooks
Elder

I look in my daughters' eyes
And I see they are not
going to suffer
They are not going to
carry the cross.

I look in my daughters' eyes
and I feel we are not alone.
"We have you, Mother,
smart, like a spider."
They are building a house
with their saliva.

"My mother followed her mother, my grandmother. She just follow. But I don't. I want to rebel. I want to change."

JEAN HUI SHIH

Jean is a soft-spoken yet granite-strong woman. When Jean first came to class, I assumed she only spoke her native Taiwanese and understood very little English. She seemed so quiet and fragile that I was afraid she would crumble when I called on her. But, like many immigrant women I came to know in the Tenderloin, she only needed a little encouragement and, like a waterfall, her image-filled stories came pouring out. Jean seemed to carry her father's poetic spirit somewhere within her and at age 60 she keeps both the artist and the small business woman vibrantly alive.

JEAN HUI SHIH

Oral History
by Nancy Deutsch

My name is Jean. It means silent, but I talk too much. Hui means wisdom. My last name, Shih, means stone. You have to be quiet, still—and you can create wisdom. Even a rock or stone can become a diamond or gold or silver.

I came from a big family. One sister and four brothers. I'm in the middle. The girl is always second. The boy always first, more important. They kill the daughters. If they don't have son, their last name—they have no more.

In my sister-in-law's family, the first child was a girl. They wanted more and more boys to come. They think the boys take care of the family when the parents are old. They had many girls. They name them, "Full," "Satisfied," "No More"—meaning, "We full. We satisfied. No more girls should come." One daughter was named "Choi Di"—calling your brother to come. They finally had one boy after seven girls. Lots of girls at that time called "Choi Di." We have a saying, "The girl spreads out, like on the water. You can never pick her up. She no use to you."

My parents pay attention more to my brothers' school, have to study hard. My mother taught me how to be housewife, care for children, husband. Of course, I didn't like doing housework. My school was a very good school, but my mother not too encouraging. We had to walk to school, get up very early, prepare rice. I had to prepare for my brothers. I would get nervous. I liked art, but no time to study.

When I was about 13 years old, I study English. My teacher, very nice lady, but she had a disease. Sometimes she just faint. Her eyes would roll back. She looked like a ghost. She would run out. She say, "Don't think I'm a ghost." After that, I hate English. I even put my English book in a box under my bed so I wouldn't see it.

We lived in the country, so we had a big, big space. My father was a country doctor. In that time every village had one doctor. A lot of people know us. My father was also a poet, a romantic. He was in a poetry society in Taiwan. They would gather together sometimes at our home. Very difficult for my mother. She had to take care all the people. My mother worked so hard. She was a midwife, she always had to go out. So, when she wasn't working, she always want to stay home.

When I was maybe 22, I first fall in love. I liked this boy, but my family don't know his family background. We worked together, for the government. He was from China. They say I cannot see him. They say, "Maybe he has more wives, in China."

I married another man, Ming, at 24. I don't want to get married. But he spoke Taiwanese and my mother could understand his language. She liked that. He was a friend of my cousin. He talked well, he liked my parents. My mother was crying. She wanted me to marry him. I give up. I feel sorry for her. I don't want to see her crying.

The marriage lasted 23 years, but I knew it wasn't right from the beginning. Every night, he go out. Sometimes, for one month, he not eat with the children, the family. After that I tell him, I warn him. He signed a loan for someone, and he lost all the family property. Sometimes he was good, but he not change. I try not to divorce. I try to change him. After 23 years, I divorce. I have three children. I have to take care of them. He vowed to change, many, many times. This time, I made up my mind. I came with my children to the United States.

I sold all my family jewelry—very cheap—to come to United States. Rings, pearl, a jade brooch that was passed on to me. I have nothing for my daughter, now. I hurt in my heart. But, then I worry that I have no money and no job. So, I sold all my jewelry.

I came to San Francisco in 1984. I taught myself to make jewelry. Nobody help me. First, I sell pottery, magnets. Then I learn to make jewelry with coins from Taiwan and knotting, traditional. Now, my stand is near Powell Street on Market Street. The area is very complicated. There's chess players, drug dealers, homeless, and tourists. I see so many things, too many things.

Some people are drunk. Sometimes, they turn over my table. The homeless people help me out. In my opinion, not all homeless are bad, they just have a bad situation. Some of them have a deep knowledge. I put some respect and trust in them. They very happy. They say, "How come this woman trust me? Nobody trust me, only you." I got lucky so far.

My daughter got married, when she was only 20 years old. I had to go back to Taiwan to get my two sons. Maybe she was lonely. Too young. She divorce. I tell myself, "I don't wanna do same way, my mother." Even if mistake, even if you not happy, you still have to keep married.

My daughter's 30 years old now. She studied at Art Academy, sculpture. I just want her to have opportunity. I don't want her to be too much under control by me. I just a voice. I just want her to have happiness. Freedom.

In my life, a lot of bad situations come. But maybe it grew my mind. I think sometimes that my mother gave me a lot of opportunities to learn. My mother protect my brothers too much. I think I'm stronger than them. My mother followed her mother, my grandmother. She just follow. But I don't. I want to rebel. I want to change.

Photograph by Kathrin Miller

MY MOTHER'S EYES

Thuy Nguyen
Age 12

I look in my mother's eyes and I see beautiful roses.
I look in my mother's eyes and I see a baby rabbit.

I look in my mother's eyes and I see a woman who is very beautiful.
I look in my mother's eyes and I see a hard-working woman.

I look in my mother's eyes and I see the Vietnamese people.
I look in my mother's eyes and we play.

ME & MOM

Sophonn Meas
Age 11

MY MOTHER'S EYES

Ana Perez
Age 14

I look in my mother's eyes and I see a sunny Nicaragua,
her beautiful beaches, and green palm trees.

I look in my mother's eyes and I see a beautiful garden,
a colorful rainbow, a fresh waterfall, a healthy green rain forest.

I look in my mother's eyes and I see a woman who has a very strong
will, a woman who is honest, a woman who likes to help everyone.

I look in my mother's eyes and I see a mature, loving mother who cares
for others, a role model, a strong woman.

I look in my mother's eyes and I see my little moles, my smile, my shyness.
I look in my mother's eyes and I see the world.

DEAR MOTHER

Ellen Gallagher
Elder

Whatever you were
Whatever you looked like,
I don't know.
I never saw you.
I do know
I had a vision all these years
Of a kind, tender, ever-loving
Woman
Who would hold me when
I was sad,
Who I could go to
when things went wrong.
You were there.
I know it
Because I always felt your
Presence.
I even wrote you
A letter from
Time
to
Time.
One time
I received
Your letter
from the
state hospital.
Your world
Was different
From mine,
But, I still
Loved you.

MY MOTHER'S EYES

Merari Castañeda
Age 11

I look in my mother's eyes and I see
a beautiful red rose
a lion playing
the Mexican volcanoes.

I look in my mother's eyes and I see
the delicious *coctel de camarón*
tostadas de ceviche
posole.

I look in my mother's eyes and I see
a woman who is hard working
a woman who is a helpful person
a woman who is funny
a smile.

MY MOTHER'S EYES

Flor Beltran
Age 12

I look in my mother's eyes and I see beauty.
I look in my mother's eyes and I see red and white roses.
I look in my mother's eyes and I see a blue and white flag
  of my *tierra* Nicaragua.
I look in my mother's eyes and I see a woman who has
  pride, honor and is generous.
I look in my mother's eyes and I see my eyes, my smile, my self.
I look in my mother's eyes and I see love.

MARILIA BROOKS AND DAUGHTER IN BRAZIL
QUINCEAÑERA

LETTER TO A PHOTOGRAPH—
QUINCEAÑERA

Marilia Brooks
Elder

Since time immemorial, Latin people celebrate girls at 15 years old. Big parties, beautiful dresses. On that day, they wear a new pair of shoes with the first small heel. Skin soft as a peach, lips pink like a bud of a rose before it opens with great splendor. It is a time when girls think the world is a paradise and they little princesses.

Celebrations start at morning with a reunion at the church of their religion, for the family only. In the evening, a party with food, music, dancing. A girl is presented to society, a beautiful future bride and mother. A little butterfly—*crisálida*—with the most gorgeous colors who one day will fly from home. Never forgetting her first day as an adult, loved by family and friends. That day, she is a *quinceañera*.

EMMA KHATSERNOVA WITH HER MOTHER IN RUSSIA

Dear Mother,

When I look at your photograph, I was thinking about your life. You are a beautiful girl and your life is happy. Today I am 70 years old and you are 94. I feel I knew you when you were young. I want to say I'm happy you are my mother. Your intelligence and culture helped me in my life. Your love and advice helped raise me, too.

I always love your brown eyes and your smart look. You always understand me and are my best friend in my life. I love you very much and want you to know you are one of the best mothers who lives in the world.

My love as ever,

Emma

LETTER TO A PHOTOGRAPH OF MY MOTHER

Emma Khatsernova
Elder

LETTER TO A PHOTOGRAPH OF MYSELF AT AGE 12

Betti Miner
Mother

Dear Betti,

I want you to know that you are on the threshold of your entrance into adulthood. You will be starting to date boys. You may meet someone at your school or church. Elvis is the "love" of your life right now, he is for me also. His music is very enjoyable to me.

I want to tell you to continue in your singing in the glee club and choir at church. Do not be so shy to let your voice soar to the heavens.

Remember Dad told you to always be a lady and "Don't let the boys take advantage of you. Someday you will be married and you want to be the beautiful bride all in white and make me proud of you."

This legacy I give to you to pass on to your children and grandchildren. Always look upon criticism and life's hard knocks with a sense of humor and be aware that life can be very cold. You may have to fight for your virtue and for your reputation to remain intact.

One last thing, God is always there for you. Don't be afraid to call on Him and thank and bless Him daily.

Love always,
Betti

**BETTI MINER
YEARBOOK PICTURE**

SHE IS THE CIRCLE OF LIFE

Anh Nguyen
Age 11

It's the year 1954 and
the month and the day
is January 12th. Loam, my
mother, has been born. She
came to this country when
I was six years old. She was
born in Hue, Vietnam. My
mother speaks Vietnamese
and a little English.

We both like music, but
we don't like the same kind.
I like rap and she likes this
Vietnamese type of classical
music. My mom reminds me
of the weather because she
changes her mind alot!
She is like the circle of life to me.

UNTITLED

Sonita Bun
Age 9

MEMORIES OF WORLD WAR II IN TAIWAN

Jean Hui Shih
Elder

Between my child and adult life, so different viewpoints about the war. When I was a child during the Second World War, Japan and America fought each other. I remember to me, in Taiwan, the war was so much fun. When the alarm "hoo, hooed," all the children would be yelling and running, they were so excited. We can finally have the candies and dried food we had saved in our backpacks for the war. Everybody stayed inside the bomb shelter with candlelight. It was like fun, a game.

Now, I'm older. The war to me is just hate. War symbolize nuclear danger, killing, pain, loveless, hopelessness, violence. War is terrible. I wish and pray the world would always be in peace, without war forever.

MEMORIES OF WORLD WAR II IN SIBERIA

Klara Taran
Elder

I remember when I was about 15 years old, I left the city with my mother and my sisters. My father was going to the army and sent a letter to my mom. He wrote, "Don't leave home. It's too dangerous." But my mom said, "I take us to Siberia."

We went to Siberia on the train and ship. It took a long time, 10 to 15 days. When we got to the city, we had one day or two days at most and then we went to the factory to work. We make potatoes and onions for the soldiers. In Siberia, the weather is cold. We had a terrible life. We ate only potatoes, no butter, nothing. We had only one bed. We slept in shifts. Some would sleep, while others worked.

When the war was over, my father came back to the Ukraine, and then all my family came back to the Ukraine.

LETTER TO A PHOTOGRAPH OF MY GRANDDAUGHTER ON HER WEDDING DAY

Lena Medvedovskaya
Elder

Dear Irina,

I want to tell you that I was very sad when you met a man from Poland. The Polish people were very bad to the Jews during WW II. Also, he was older than your 18 years. He was 36. I told you to change your mind. But you didn't and you married him. You told me that you loved him. It was years ago.

Now, you live in another state and have a good job. Your son is three years old. You tell me that you have a happy family.

I think I was wrong when I told you not to marry him.

Your grandmother,

Lena

ME AND MOM

Sita Meas
Age 9

MY MOTHER LOVED LAVENDER

Marilia Brooks
Elder

My mother loved lavender. All her clothes, her room, and herself always smelled of lavender. She had her clothes and lavender cologne brought to her from São Paulo, the state capital.

Everything at that time in Brazil was imported from France and Germany. Lavender sachets were very much in fashion to perfume girls' trousseaus.

My grandmother gave her a trunk made with the best wood that smells of cedar of Libano. There my mother kept the linens all embroidered by herself. And there were the lavender sachets.

I remember my mother after her bath and the sweet smell of her. She was so lovely. Although she died when I was a young child of seven, I do not forget her.

CINNAMON CALLED ME BACK

Jean Hui Shih
Elder

Cinnamon called me back
to my childhood. I always like
anything that tastes or smells
like cinnamon. When I was a little girl,
I liked to gather with two or three friends
and run into the forest near the village
where I lived. We played inside and
searched for cinnamon trees.

Amazing, we can identify which
is cinnamon tree, then just peel
the skin and eat it. The taste
is so good and strong, sometimes
my tears drop it is so strong.

JEAN HUI SHIH AND HER MOTHER IN TAIWAN

Many times as I went boldly forward with my lesson plan, I'd stop myself and try to imagine what it would be like to leave the United States due to war, famine, or poverty; be dropped into a crime-ridden neighborhood; and have to learn another language and culture at age 6 or 16 or 76. The diverse worlds these women and girls straddled seemed at times unfathomable. Writing about their "roots" was one way to link these worlds. The selections included here explore the roots of cultural and female identity that tie these women—young and old—to their past and sustain them in their future.

CHAPTER FIVE

"I Have Nicaragua's Rivers in My Hair, Long and Loose Like the Water…"

MASSIEL

Photograph by Flor Beltran
Age 12

I have my mother's energy of not getting tired
I have my *abuela* Lisa's ways of telling jokes
I have Nicaragua's rivers in my hair
Long and loose like the water
But, my imagination takes me anywhere.

MY ROOTS

Massiel Perez
Age 12

GIRLS' WRITING CLASS

Journal Entry
by Nancy Deutsch

Tonight in class I asked the girls to write about experiences of discrimination. Most of them were fogging over and I knew I had about five seconds before they'd trade me for chips and soda at the corner store. "OK," I said, "list all the names you've ever been called that you didn't like." One story after the other came pouring out. Flor said, "A boy in my school calls me 'Mexican Girl,' even though I'm from Nicaragua." Diana, who's Chinese, told us, "They call me 'Yellow Dirt.'" Flor started writing on the board for a group poem. Massiel, whom I call "The Director," was shouting an opening rhyming stanza she had created instantly. "Read what Flor wrote on the board first," I told her in an attempt to organize chaos. Then Irina, one of the moms, wandered in. She insisted the poem have a rhythm and tapped out their lyrics in her heavy Moscow accent and black leather boots. The girls are giggling uncontrollably at this point. Luckily, Irina was oblivious, lost in the beat. Our defiant group poem, "Don't Call Me That!" became a mix of rap and a Russian drill team chant.

DON'T CALL ME THAT

Group Poem by Girls' Writing Class
Ana, Aireen, Amy, Angela,
Diane, Flor, Felicia,
Massiel, Romany, Ruby,
Sita, Sophie, Sophonn,
Tina, and Violeta
Ages 9–17

Don't call me this, don't call me that
If it was you, you wouldn't like it like that.

Don't call me punk, I ain't a skunk
Don't tell me that Cambodians suck.

Don't call me butterscotch, don't call me Oreo
Call me my name, so there's no one to blame.

Don't call me slant eyes, don't call me yellow dirt
Don't call me names 'cause it really hurts.

Just because I'm Latina, doesn't mean I'm Mexican
Just because I'm Filipina, doesn't mean I'm Chinese.

So, be polite, don't get in a fight
It doesn't matter if you're black or white.

It doesn't matter if you're woman or man
Let's get together and all hold hands.

It doesn't matter where you come from
Let's get together and show some love.

Make a friend of a different race
Let's all treat each other the same.

Don't call me this, don't call me that
If it was you, you wouldn't like it like that.

Let's not hate, let's collaborate!

"Once I went to the store to buy some bread and I got caught in a crossfire. They started shooting and I had to go hide with my daughter Angela behind a basket."
MILAGRO ZAMORA

Milagro is a determined, protective mother of four daughters and a son. She and her husband escaped war-torn Nicaragua in the late '70s during a bloody civil war between the brutal Somoza dictatorship and the Sandinista Liberation Front. I would often pass Milagro on the street in my neighborhood after she escorted her youngest daughter Isabel on the 30-minute bus ride from the Tenderloin to her elementary school in the Mission. Although Milagro hadn't slept yet—having worked at a bakery across the bay until 3:00 a.m.—she made sure her daughter got to school safely. Unfortunately, her bright, young daughter attended one of the city's worst schools, and I would cringe imagining Isabel there after all her mother's efforts. Milagro's two older daughters now attend community college and her dream is that all of her children will someday follow this path. Due to the danger Milagro faced in leaving her country, she asked that neither her photo nor her real name be revealed.

MILAGRO ZAMORA

Oral History
by Nancy Deutsch
Translated from Spanish
by her daughter

My mother died from a miscarriage. My grandmother told me this when I was 12 years old. When we were little and we would ask for our mother, my grandmother would say, "She's gonna come one day." When I would ask her questions, she would stay quiet and then sometimes I would see her cry.

I grew up in Managua, Nicaragua. I was born in 1953. I was young [under President Somoza], but at one school the soldiers came and said that one of the boys studying there was a problem with the government. The soldiers smashed up the whole school. In the night, they were still looking around and went through everything. You could hear people crying because there were gunshots. They would hit innocent people to scare them.

I was visiting my brother one day, when the soldiers took over the neighborhood. They were knocking on doors and they had their faces covered. When they opened the door, the soldiers would have a knife in their guns. They wanted the young boys from the houses.

In front of the house, I saw they lined up a bunch of boys. They were asking for information. There were kids outside and they were going to shoot all of them. They didn't care who they shot. But then, they put them in the jeep and drove away. I didn't know where they took them. They might kill them or torture them.

Once I went to the store to buy some bread and I got caught in a crossfire. They [the soldiers] started shooting and I had to go hide with my daughter Angela behind a basket. I had to go back home, so I picked up Angela and left all the groceries. I lifted her up so they could see her. She was three years old and I was pregnant. They followed me in a car, until I got home. When I would hear the shooting my toes would roll up.

We felt in between the Somozistas and the Sandinistas. If we talked to someone who was a Sandinista, Somoza might kill us. If we talked to someone who was a Somozista, the Sandinistas might kill us. I wanted peace and I wanted the Sandinistas to bring peace. The people didn't know what they were gonna do, they [the Sandinistas] were new to us.

We found a lawyer who gave us a permit to leave the country. He told us we could take a few little things and some food for the trip. We were escaping. We were fugitives. We went to Guatemala and then Mexico. Rosa was twelve, Gabriela nine, Angela was seven, Carlos was five, and Isabel was three years old.

They tried to stop us at the Mexican border, but I told them our story. They said our papers were not completely in order. I told the Mexican guards, "If we go back they will kill us for escaping, so go ahead and kill us—we're not going back."

We went to *una casa de refugiados,* a house for refugees. The people there treated us very well. They gave us some papers to take to immigration to make our passports legal. They told us that we could get legal help and could apply for political asylum. My husband was given a permit to work, but not a green card. When we came to the United States we looked for a lawyer and became political refugees.

I would like to become a citizen, but I can't go to classes because I have to work. I work in a factory. It's very hot. We have to iron a thousand pieces in one hour. Immigrants take the worst jobs, the jobs nobody else will take. But, I do it for my children. So they have a future.

I went through secondary school, like the eighth grade. I liked math and science best. I wanted to be a doctor. I would like my daughters to study medicine, my son to study construction. Something they like, so they make a good career for the future. If not medicine, maybe a teacher or something to help children. I want them to study hard. I wish them to help the family, to make better the family.

I don't like the [Tenderloin] area. Too many people with drugs. I worry that something bad will happen to my children. I don't like this neighborhood, but I like this building and all the programs. It's beautiful. Since I work, I don't have time to go to all the programs, but they tell me what they do in [the writing] class. I wrote poems in school, but I was too shy to read them out loud. I would like my daughters to do something like this. Helping children. Teaching children to do better. I wish them the best.

MY ROOTS

Felicia Copeland
Age 12

I have my mother's looks and personality
my grandmother's wisdom and power
my auntie's attitude when I get mad.

I have the color of the goldfish scales in my eyes
the shyness of a sunflower hiding in the shade
the strength to earn my goals
the courage to fly with wings of my own.

MY ROOTS

Flor Beltran
Age 11

I have grandmother Maria's energy
my grandmother Mimi's name
my mother's brownish-green eyes
my Tia Lia's intelligence.

I have the fish's swimming power
the volcanoes of Nicaragua
the beauty of a red rose
but, my writing is all my own.

Photograph by Kathrin Miller

**FLOR BELTRAN
IN COURTYARD**

RACISM IS LIKE A KNIFE

Ruby Marucut
Age 10

Racism is like a bad lion.
It is like a stormy day.
Racism is when children fight.
Racism is when people get mad.
Racism is just dumb and a bad thing to the world.
Racism is like a very sharp cactus.
It is like a knife poking you.

RACISM IS LIKE KILLING WITHOUT WEAPONS

Maria Powers
Age 12

Racism is like a dark cloud over the world.
It is like a room with no light, no love, no peace.
Racism is like thunder and lightning.
It is a war with no end.
Racism is like killing without weapons.
Racism is like a BIG BOMB.
Racism kills you.

MY HAIR

Ashley Adams
Age 9

MEMOIRS/PERSPECTIVES FROM BLACK GIRLHOOD TO BLACK WOMANHOOD

Winona Addison
Mother

Little black girl am i
  bad, ugly, nappy hair have i.

In the kitchen gettin' it fried,
  "Fried, dyed, laid to the side."
    Bergamot oil, sweet charred sense of smell

      CRACKLE, SNAP, POP
Red, hot, metal claws, gripping from the root
    steamed heat,
      Seeping,
        SWEEPING,
          through my scalp
        NAPPY hair
          Bad hair
        NATURALLY STRAIGHT hair—The forbidden fruit.

Birthdays, holidays, first day of school
    Big, thick bang across my forehead long.
      It was cool and usually
          the rule.

But as i listen to the soft memories echo loud,

    "Girl sit still and get your hair done
        before you get burnt."

      we HAD NO VOICE
          i
      HAD NO CHOICE

    But to sit in that kitchen
      and listen to my hair fry

        and listen to my lonely painful cry

"When I grow up, I ain't neva gonna press my hair."
        and NOW. . .
BLACK WOMAN   am I,
    GOOD, BEAUTIFUL, UNIQUE, CREATIVE hair,
          have I.

DON'T

Violeta Perez
Age 18
Aireen Bulante
Age 12

Don't judge me by my skin
Don't judge me by my race
Judge me by who I am
A person without hate.

I'm just another Filipino
Mixed with Latino
That's mad at the world
Because of the pressure it makes
Being in a world full of hate.

As I walk through the streets
Of San Francisco I see people
Fighting because of hate.
I try to stop them, but I can't 'cause
What they're thinking about is hate.

As I walk through the street
I see people staring at me
As if I were just another piece
Of garbage laying in the street.
But what they don't know
Is the real me
A girl with a future ahead
A girl that's sweet.

So, don't judge me by my race
Language or face
After death we will all become
The same
No hate will separate us
Ever again.

RESIST 187

Photograph by Jenny Saechang
Age 12

MY ROOTS

Ruby Rose Marucut
Age 11

I have my grandmother Samonte's hair
my mother's attitude
aunt Myrna's eyes
the fish's movement
the name of a flower
the Philippines' spirit.
but my attitude,
feelings,
and imagination
are all my own.

I AM A WOMAN WHO

Marilia Brooks
Elder

I am a woman who loves birds,
because they can fly, they are free.
I am a woman who wants to be a bird
and not need a passport.
I am a woman who is like a white hyacinth,
that smells wonderful and perfumes all the
women in the world.
I am a woman who is very romantic
and vulnerable.
I am a woman who is always looking
for happiness moving like a gypsy,
from country to country
looking for the miracle of finding myself.
I am a woman who suffered much,
but still believes in love.

KLARA AND DAVID TARAN IN THE UKRAINE

DO YOU MISS ME, CHERKASSY?

Klara Taran
Elder

I asked Cherkassy,
"Do you miss me?"
I miss you. I miss my city.
The river Dnepr is fine.
I left you seven years ago.

I asked Cherkassy her
favorite color.
"Red," she answered.
The food in Ukraine
is very good.
A lot of vegetable, fruit,
cheese, milk, beef.

In the summer, it is hot.
In the winter, it is cold.
I miss my city.
Ya ostavila tam moyu dushu.
I leave my soul.

I TOLD BRAZIL

Marilia Brooks
Elder

I told Brazil,
"I love you, your sky,
your sea, and my friends.

Leaving you is like leaving
a part of my soul.
My heart is bleeding.

But I lost my love,
my house, and my
dreams were shattered.

I am leaving to America
the only country I love
the same as I love you."

Brazil, with that enormous
heart, he always had told me,
"Go, be happy

find a new way of life
but please do not forget
that I love you."

I AM A WOMAN BETWEEN

Lena Medvedovskaya
Elder

I am a woman between Leningrad and the USA.
I am a woman between Russian and English.
I am a woman between Russian theater and the opera *Carmen*.
I am a woman between the river Dnepr and the Pacific Ocean.

I AM A WOMAN

Jean Hui Shih
Elder

I am a woman who came from Taipei, Taiwan.
I am a woman now living in San Francisco.
I am a woman living in the Tenderloin where
there is a drug and alcohol area.
I am a woman who is a street artist on
Market Street where it is dirty, crowded, noisy.
I am a woman who loves to go to the ocean
to balance my mood, like a car tune-up, refresh my system.
I am a woman whose name means wisdom.
I am a woman who tries to be faithful even standing in the rain
I still try to stand up
And be still.

"Dear Mr. Mayor, Please Write Back 'Cause I Live In A Bad Neighborhood"

CHAPTER SIX

For weeks we worked on our "Dear Mr. Mayor" letter/poems after learning that San Francisco's mayor, Willie Brown, would visit the Tenderloin. This could be a real chance for the girls to use the power of poetry to share their hopes and dreams for the community. The day finally came and over 100 people had gathered. Ana, a shy but poised Latina with striking black eyes, looked up from her paper, stared into the mayor's eyes and spoke the final line of her poem—"P.S. When you were 14 years old like me, what did you want to be when you grew up?" The longing behind her question seemed to stop time. The room went silent. Then the mayor led the audience in applause. For that brief moment, it seemed like some true connection was made. Ana's voice had been heard. Her poem, like the others here, pleads with us not to forget her fragile dream of a better life, a better neighborhood, a better world.

ANA PEREZ

Photograph by Ruby Marucut
Age 12

Dear Mr. Mayor,

What if all children had a safe neighborhood where they could walk with their heads up and feel safe at all times instead of walking with their heads down looking over their shoulders, watching out for themselves?
What if all grown-ups had their own homes, jobs, more respect for their kids? Then this world would be safer, there would be more jobs and no homeless people dying in the streets.

Love always,
Ana

P.S. When you were 14 years old like me, what did you want to be when you grew up?

DEAR MR. MAYOR

Ana Perez
Letter to Mayor
Age 14

GRADUATION NIGHT

Journal Entry
by Nancy Deutsch

Last night I went to Violeta's graduation. I was honored to be invited and thrilled to hear her friends cheer as she crossed the stage to accept her diploma. Afterwards, some of the parents rented limos for the night so their graduates could cruise around San Francisco in pomp and circumstance. Violeta's mother and father took the bus and treated Violeta, her younger sister Massiel, and me to the extravagance of cab ride back to the Tenderloin. Violeta seemed melancholy and quiet on the ride home. I wondered if the distance between the red velvet auditorium curtains and the gritty streets of the Tenderloin was taking its toll. Then, all in one breath, Massiel blurted out that she got an "A" on her class project on bulimia and that a woman was shot just outside their building a few nights ago. "Nobody came to help her! We could hear her moan," Massiel told me as the cab pulled up to Jones Street.

These are the daily battlefields of the Tenderloin. Some days I worry that I'll be the next casualty—unable to help carry their stories and shoulder the pain. I wonder where they find the strength to step into the streets each day and I fear for their future. But then, Jean Hui will bring the women's class tiger's-eye earrings she's made for good luck, Flor will tell me she won a video by entering a poetry contest, and I'll hear a rumor that Violeta has applied to nursing school. And somehow, we'll all be laughing again in class when I ask the elders to write about their dreams for the neighborhood. Lena, in her Leningrad accent, will say, "My dream is that my husband comes back to life," and another elder will answer, "For me, that would be a nightmare."

Dear Mr. Mayor,

What if all children had the freedom to enjoy their childhood and not waste it on drugs, murder, and death? What if all grown-ups had a good heart and worked to stop Proposition 187 that's trying to get rid of all the immigrants? Then, this world would be the Promised Land that God told us about, full of milk and honey.

Love,
Violeta

P.S. I hope you will do something really soon, before this world comes to an end, full of violence and hate.

DEAR MR. MAYOR

Violeta Perez
Age 18

Dear Governor,

I am a woman who immigrated from Russia. I am a woman who believes that the USA cannot take aging people's SSI. I am a woman who likes culture and American national tradition. I am a woman who studied citizenship test and passed it. I am a woman who has the oldest mother, 93 years old, she passed citizenship test too. Our family likes America and forever remember she gives us house, food, and happy life.

Sincerely,
Emma Khatsernova

DEAR GOVERNOR

Emma Khatsernova
Elder

Photograph by Kathrin Miller

"The children are actually more Americans than Mexicans... What can I do in Mexico? My life now is here... All our hopes are here."

ESPERANZA CASTEÑEDA

Esperanza was one of the most active and involved mothers I met while working in the Tenderloin. Every potluck, every party, every intergenerational class held for the mothers, daughters, and elders—Esperanza was there with at least one of her three daughters in tow and always with her delicious gelatina de leche. *She was also one of the few mothers able to squeeze out the time to be a community activist. Esperanza attended endless meetings at her church to help stop Proposition 187, which threatened to cut off education and health care for the children of undocumented immigrants. With her shy smile and gentle tenacity Esperanza passes on the legacy of her name to her daughters—hope.*

ESPERANZA CASTEÑEDA

Oral History
Translated from Spanish
by Marilia Brooks

I came to this country in 1992, because my husband was living in California for two years. Where we lived in Jalisco, Mexico, the factories closed and there wasn't any work. My husband lost his job. He painted boats and Lake Chapala was dry. He came to America looking for a better life and a better job. He got a job painting boats in Sausalito.

Nobody stopped us from coming in [to this country]. I have heard that Central American people or Chinese people come in boats and it takes them two or three months to get here or some of them just die. But I had no trouble. When we came, we had friends from Mexico who lived in the Tenderloin. We lived in a small studio apartment with nine people. I felt like a prisoner.

In 1993 we moved into 111 Jones. I like the building, but the people around the building I don't like. People are doing drugs in front of the children. They have a bad life in the streets and my children see things they shouldn't have to see. They say, "Mommy, what is it?" I answer them the best way I can, but I don't want to shock the children telling too much the truth. Sometimes, I say, "Maybe they are sick, for that reason they have the needles." In Mexico, you don't see people injecting themselves with drugs or in every little corner using drugs. There's more people homeless here in California than in Mexico.

It was very hard for me to leave my sisters and brothers and come to America because we are ten in our family. Seven still live in Mexico. I came looking for a better life, especially for the children, and a good job for my husband.

In the '40s, my father came to America for work. He couldn't take the children and my mother because of ten children. We were separated. My mother was just a housewife and we lived on the money my father made working in America.

I had five sisters and four brothers. I used to hang around with my sisters. My brothers were older. In Mexico, the boys don't do a lot around the house, only the women. Now I don't think that's very good. Both the female and the male should have the same amount of work.

My mom expected me to study and do my homework before we could go out and play. When I was young I wanted to be a teacher, but then I realized it was too hard and too long. Then I started to learn to be a secretary, because I thought it was shorter. When we were young, our mom let us choose what we wanted to be. Now, I'm trying my best to learn English and do something for the future. For me it's very difficult, but still I have hope. I like to study very much.

I have three daughters, 13, 10, and 4.

Photograph by Kathrin Miller

In Mexico, I didn't have many hopes for my daughters. But, here, my children can speak two languages and if they study, they could have a very good future. My oldest daughter wants to be a teacher, the second one loves art, and the baby wants to be a firefighter. [laughs]

I encourage my daughters to stay in school so that when they grow up they have good jobs. Not like other people that didn't continue with their studies and now they just clean houses or are janitors. My advice is to study so when you grow up you can be something big or something good.

In two more years, my daughter will have a *quinceañera*. Fifteen years is a big celebration. It starts with a beautiful Mass. She becomes a señorita, a woman. The best I can do for my daughter at 15 is to give a good example and show her how bad is that life for the girls [prostitutes] in the Tenderloin and avoid all the worst.

I belong to St. Boniface Church, around the corner. We're working on something for people who are not legal residents. The church is helping all the immigrants become citizens and to fight any law against it, like Proposition 187. In 187 they say they want to take the children of immigrants from school. It's not right. We are working to help the people become citizens, to avoid the children having to leave school. If they [the parents] become a citizen, they have more rights and it's much, much better for them.

I am now very, very happy, because we have all the papers, all the permission to stay in America. But, I am very much concerned about my friends and other people who have a different situation. All my friends tell me about that, how they are afraid, how they need help. What can I do? I want to do something.

I felt humiliation [with Proposition 187] and was very, very afraid if they do something against the immigrants—especially from Mexico, because really they need help. People are very afraid of having to leave America. It's terrible for the children.

The children are actually more Americans than Mexicans. They were born here. They know the language already. They go to school, they are good students. They are American citizens in a very good way! What can I do in Mexico? My life now is here, my family is here. All our hopes are here.

HANDS

Photograph by Violeta Perez
Age 18

Dear Mr. Mayor,

What if all children had good homes and good families?
What if all grown-ups had jobs and money?
Then this world would be a circle of hope.

Love,
Jenny

P.S. Have you ever been to Thailand?

DEAR MR. MAYOR

Jenny Saechang
Age 12

Dear Mr. Mayor,

What if all children had books to read to encourage themselves? What if all grown-ups had money to buy clothes and food to eat and always get to see their children every day after work? Then this world will be more meaningful and happier.

Love,
Stephanie

P.S. Have you ever wanted something you couldn't have?

DEAR MR. MAYOR

Stephanie Phan
Age 12

DEAR MR. MAYOR

Ruby Marucut
Age 12

Dear Mr. Mayor,

What if all children had a neighborhood with no drug dealers?
What if all women and men could live a better life
with no arguing or fighting?
Then all kids and grown-ups could have a happy life.

Love,
Ruby

P.S. I hope you like poetry.

DEAR MR. MAYOR

F. Copeland
Age 12

Dear Mr. Mayor,

What if all children had food every day?
What if all grown-ups had more money every day?
Then this world would be a wonderful place.

Love,
F. Copeland

P.S. This is our home!

GIRLS IN COURTYARD

Photograph by Kathrin Miller

DEAR GOVERNOR

Jean Hui Shih
Elder

Dear Governor,

I know your name only a few years ago. I had a test for American citizen. The first examination question to me is, "Who is the California governor?" From that time on I started to pay attention to you, either on TV or the news.

Most of the immigrant, except rich people or criminals, works very hard in this country. Culture, language, and customs all very different, therefore those making very little in a more difficult living position.

I don't know anything about political. But, do not attack too much for us. Please, don't break our American dream.

Sincerely,
Jean Hui Shih

Photograph by Felicia Copeland

DEAR MR. MAYOR

Felicia Copeland
Age 12

Dear Mr. Mayor,

What if all children had a cure for HIV and a home for helpless children?
What if there was no racism and everybody was equal?
What if all grown-ups had respect for all and weren't so abusive
and no men were raping?
What if all grown-ups had a good neighborhood with no disrespect?
What if we had more recreation to keep kids off the streets and out of trouble?
Then we could have a good neighborhood for the elders and
make everything safe.

Love,
Felicia

P.S. Please write back 'cause I live in a bad neighborhood.

Photograph by Kathrin Miller

If anything got saved this year, it was the old ragged bougainvillea bush in back of McDonald's hamburger joint at 7th and Market. The bush was much like the neighborhood—dirty, unkempt, smelly, neglected, and starving for a handout. A cup of water now and then.

There was and still is an old man who loves that bush. He sees that it gets water secretly at night from an abandoned building faucet. One night, I had seen him trying to tie up the tree where it had fallen into McAllister Street. Later, my friend Ron and I, from the Dorothy Day Community, visited the manager and told them about their neglected old bush. Could they allow us to tie it up and give it some water? They agreed and even helped us.

Well, it has grown helter-skelter. It is so tall now and so clean, the veins of the leaves are a joy to look at. On my walk every evening for my newspaper, I visit the tree, say "hello" and tell it how proud I am of its endurance. I tell it how it is truly an inspiration to me. Surviving hard times.

The view out my seventh floor window to the Tenderloin is the greatest. When I look out and down on that bush, I'm happy and sometimes I think it waves back to me.

SURVIVING HARD TIMES

Ellen Gallagher
Elder

CHILDREN IN COURTYARD

Photograph by Kathrin Miller

WHEN I WAS YOUNG

Arwa Farhan
Mother

When I was young, I had to wear a veil.
Now that I'm older and moved to the United States,
I no longer wear the veil.

When I was young, I helped my sister care for her children.
Now that I'm older, I care for my own children.

When I was young, I liked to sew dresses.
Now that I'm older I make three dresses a day.

When I was young, I liked to swim.
Now that I'm older, I still enjoy going to the beach
when there are no people around.

When I was young I was very close to my sister, Saida.
Now that I'm older, I'm still very close to my sister whom
I love very much.

When I was young, I wanted to be married so I could
wear makeup, a nice dress, and go outside.
Now that I'm older, I can walk alone in the Tenderloin.

When I was young, I wanted to be a throaty singer.
Now that I'm older, I still try my voice at Sunday hymns.

When I was young, I wanted to be Joan Crawford, then later, a nun.
Now that I'm older, I go to church every Sunday.

When I was young, I wanted to be a housewife.
Now that I'm older, I want more freedom and to be independent.

When I was young, I wanted to dance and play the piano.
Now that I'm older, I still want to.

When I was young, I wanted to run out of the gates
of the orphanage and on to freedom.
Now that I'm older, I grasp where that freedom took me.

When I was young, I wanted to go first to Costa Rica,
then to the United States.
Now that I'm older, I want to go back to Nicaragua.

When I was young I wanted to go to Japan.
Now, that I'm older I want to stay in the United States.

When I was young, I wanted to not be so skinny.
Now that I'm older, I am just like everyone else
and want to be a little slimmer.

When I was young I was self-conscious,
no encouraging words, too scared to sing.
Now that I'm older, I wonder how I survived it all.

WHEN I WAS YOUNG

Group poem by Women's Writing Class
Adelle, Betti, Ellen, Emma,
Jean, Klara and Yolanda
Ages 53–74

Photograph by Kathrin Miller

**KLARA TARAN AND
EMMA KHATSERNOVA
IN COURTYARD**

DREAMS FOR MY NEIGHBORHOOD

Emma Khatsernova
Elder

In my dreams I see mothers
who never bury their sons.

In my dreams I see an earth
with no borders.

In my dreams I see all races
and colors together.

In my dreams I can fly to Japan.

In my dreams I can stay home
and take care of my mother forever.

DREAMS FOR MY NEIGHBORHOOD

Jean Hui Shih
Elder

In my dreams
I see children
who are pure and never lie,
mothers
who are always full of love
in their eyes.

In my dreams
I see an earth growing
more green
different races, cultures,
and customs living together.

In my dreams,
I see a big hill I was climbing
so hard, but still

a long way to go,
I can never end.

In my dreams
I can fly over a big lake, bright
and warm between a lovely
house and me.
I am swimming
to a clean, quiet peace.

In my dreams
I have
a lot
of
stories.

DREAMS FOR MY NEIGHBORHOOD

Lena Medvedovskaya
Elder

In my dreams
I see children who are happy
and don't know the difference
between the colors of the skin,
I see mothers who never have to wait
for their sons to come home from the war.

In my dreams
I see myself in a beautiful garden
with many flowers,
I can fly to the moon on vacation,
I know English and can understand TV.

In my dreams
my husband can come back,
my children are having a happy life,
I am young again and didn't make
too many mistakes.

LENA MEDVEDOVSKAYA IN LENINGRAD, AGE 16

MY HANDS

Group poem
by Women's Writing Class
Betti, Ellen, Jean,
Marilia and Yolanda
Ages 53–74

My hands pull the covers
My hands open the doors
My hands put out the light for the night.

My hands held my first doll, a new unnamed baby, a bottle of goat's milk
My hands held my first lipstick, which I hid from my grandmother
My hands held a piece of silk, a needle
for stitching rich people's pillowcases.

My hands do something good for me
My hands do something very stupid
My hands wear a green diamond ring
I bought in a pawn shop in the Mission.

My hands opened my first book
My hands raised my daughter
My hands nursed people to health.

My hands held my first and only corsage
My hands painted my first picture
My hands pray to the Blessed Mother.

My hands are ugly because they work all the time
My hands move easily like slick dancing legs
My hands are getting old before my time.

My hands stroke my granddaughter's face
My hands hold the pen that puts poetry on paper
My hands brush back my hair when I am weary
at the end of the day.

My hands are old now
Now, they are resting
I need you, my hands.

My hands carry all the past.

Photograph by Kathrin Miller

About the Author
Nancy Deutsch has conducted poetry, journal writing, and oral history programs for over fifteen years. She's currently an Artist in Residence directing poetry and intergenerational programs in the public schools and low-income housing. Nancy received her M.S.S.W. from the University of Wisconsin and worked for many years counseling women and teaching women's studies. She and her partner live with their son in San Francisco, California.

About the Photographer
Kathrin Miller is an award-winning photographer. Her work has appeared in *Newsweek*, *Time*, *Parenting*, *The Utne Reader*, *The L.A. Times* and *The Tenderloin Times*. She and her partner have two daughters and reside in San Francisco, California.

Additional copies of *Voices of Our Own* are available through your local bookstore or through From My Window Books for $24.95 plus postage and handling. Also available: *Voices of Our Own: Helping Mothers, Daughters and Elders Tell Their Stories.* This 100-page, step-by-step training manual is available for $20.00 plus postage and handling.

To order, contact:
From My Window Books
c/o Nancy Deutsch
267 Fair Oaks Street
San Francisco, CA 94110
email: nancydeutsch@earthlink.net

INDEX TO AUTHORS AND ARTISTS

Adams, Ashley   25, 46, 80
Addison, Winona   45, 53, 81
Alonzo, Rossana   36
Amado, Victoria   26–28
Arguero, Benita   29
Beltran, Flor   15, 18, 29, 30, 47, 52, 63, 73, 79
Berry, Mia   23
Bove, Yolanda   34
Brooks, Marilia   57, 64, 70, 83, 84
Bulante, Aireen   39, 82
Bun, Sonita   67
Castañeda, Esperanza   36, 90–92
Castañeda, Merari   52, 63
Castañeda, Siomara   36
Copeland, Donisha   37
Copeland, Felicia   10, 45, 48, 55, 79, 96
Eat, Tina   14
Farhan, Arwa   35, 98
Gallagher, Ellen   5, 16, 25, 62, 97
Hui Shih, Jean   7, 48, 58–60, 68, 71
Jones, Anita   2
Khatsernova, Emma   31, 65, 89, 99, 100
Khorn, Ciceila   13
Lee, Diana   48
Lewis, Venitta   8–10
Maptynov, Sura   35
Marucut, Ruby   12, 47, 50, 55, 80, 83, 87, 94
McDonald, Myrna   11, 46
McLeod, Bill   20
Meas, Sita   12, 70
Meas, Sophonn   61
Meas, Ven Yem   42–44
Medvedovskaya, Lena   51, 69, 85, 101
Miner, Betti   20, 57, 66
Nguyen, Anh   30, 41, 67
Nguyen, Linda   32
Nguyen, Thuy   61
Panaligan, Janelle   23
Perez, Ana   12, 18, 61, 87
Perez, Massiel   73
Perez, Violeta   33, 47, 82, 89, 93
Phan, Stephanie   37, 93
Pierce, Adelle   16
Powers, Maria   80
Saechang, Jenny   82, 93
Soun, Loura   32
Tana, Sophia   31
Taran, Klara   49, 68, 84, 99
Urbina, Nidia   31
Yaeger, Gwen   35
Zamora, Angela   39
Zamora, Milagro   76–78